THE *Magna Book* OF

~

TEDDY BEARS

~

A TREASURED COLLECTION
OF OUR FAVOURITE
CHILDHOOD TOY

Editor: Jo Finnis

Designer: Claire Leighton (original design concept: Peter Bridgewater, Nigel Duffield)

Photographer: Neil Sutherland

Researchers: Roseanne Eckart; Leora Kahn

Production: Gerald Hughes, Ruth Arthur, Sally Connolly, Andrew Whitelaw, Neil Randles

Typesetting: Julie Smith

Acknowledgements

Special thanks to The London Toy and Model Museum
for allowing photography of teds and memorabilia.

Bettmann Archive: p.15, 18, 32; Granada Television: p.36-37; Tom Hall: p.9; Fozzie Bear,
courtesy Jim Henson Productions, Inc. © 1977. All rights reserved. p.39;
London Toy and Model Museum: p.10, 11, 12, 13, 16, 17, 19, 20, 22, 23,
24, 25, 26, 27, 30, 35, 38, 43, 44, 45, 47, 48, 52, 55, 56, 59;
New York Public Library: p.33; Rupert Bear Illustration p.30-31 courtesy Express Newspapers plc;
Paddington Bear illustration by Peggy Fortnum from *A Bear Called Paddington* published by HarperCollins
Children's Books, courtesy Ms Fortnum; Paddington Bear p.35 courtesy Copyrights, Milton, Oxford;
photograph of Jeremy Irons and Anthony Andrews p.36-37 from *Brideshead Revisited* courtesy Hulton
Management and Peters, Fraser and Dunlop, © Granada Television.

Lines from "Teddy Bear" from *When We Were Very Young* copyright A.A. Milne under the Berne Convention
reproduced by the permission of Curtis Brown Limited, London and Methuen Children's Books;
Copyright 1924 by E.P. Dutton, renewed 1952 by A.A. Milne. Used by permission of
Dutton Children's Books, a division of Penguin Books USA Inc.
Extract from *Summoned by Bells* by Sir John Betjeman courtesy John Murray (Publishers) Ltd.
Extract from *Brideshead Revisited* courtesy Peters, Fraser and Dunlop.
"Teddy Bears' Picnic" © 1907, M. Whitmark and Sons USA. Reproduced by permission of
B. Feldman and Co. Ltd, London WC2H 0EA.

Thanks to Sampson and the gang in the Hug.

THE *Magna Book* OF

TEDDY BEARS

HAMISH MACGILLIVRAY

MAGNA
BOOKS

$\mathcal{W}$ild $\mathcal{B}$ear

Today, bears are generally regarded as cuddly mammals. In the past, however, they were believed to be ferocious beasts with supernatural powers. With its large body, thick fur and powerful clawed limbs, the bear became a god for pagan tribes living in the forests of Europe, Asia and America. From the Vikings in Scandinavia to the Ainu tribes in Japan, the bear became a symbol of strength and resurrection. The pagan respect for bears disappeared with the rise of the Christians. The early Christian church was convinced that the bear was such a cruel creature that it had to be a reincarnation of the Devil.

Bears might have scared people, but it did not stop the capture and killing of these animals for barbaric spectator sports. The Romans enjoyed the bloody shows of dogs attacking and baiting chained bears in amphitheatres. Bear baiting became so popular in Europe that baiting was staged in special bear gardens.

Right: *The American Black Bear is generally only dangerous when he loses his fear of humans through familiarity.*

First Toys

From the Middle Ages to the Victorian era, captive bears were forced to perform tricks on street corners or fairs. The first toy bears were small figures carved out of wood, many produced for toy Noah's Arks. In the 1750s, two-dimensional flat tin figures of performing bears became available. Most of these toys were manufactured by cottage industries in southern Germany. From the 16th century, German toys were exported up the Rhine river to the rest of Europe.

Bears were traditionally hunted for their meat and hides. During the 19th century, the practice was elevated to a sport for the rich and famous, and the bear became a popular victim for big game hunters. At the same time, a strange fascination with them persisted, which inspired folk stories and, in turn, toys.

Right: *Little and large carved wooden bears c.1850s (London Toy and Model Museum).*

Below: *A performing bear and owner made out of flat tin plate c.1800 (London Toy and Model Museum).*

Moving Toys

In the forests of northern Europe, there were many stories about Mishka the bear or Bruin the bear. In the 17th century, Bruin appeared in the Dutch children's story of 'Reynard the Fox'. Bears made frequent appearances in the growth of children's books in the 1800s, for example *Goldilocks and the Three Bears* and *Grimms' Fairy Tales*.

In the 19th century, the Bruin became a large push-and-pull children's toy bear with wheels attached to its legs. For the adult market, there was a demand for automaton clockwork bears made in Germany and France. By 1890, the automaton bears could smoke, drink or perform tricks for the amusement of inebriated dinner guests.

Despite these popular toys and stories, bears of the wild were still regarded as terrifying animals. It was in 1902 that the image of the bear was transformed for all time.

Left: *A clockwork drinking bear, dating from the 1890s (London Toy and Model Museum).*

Below: *A large Bruin on wheels, made by Steiff in 1910 (London Toy and Model Museum).*

13

Teddy's Bear

In 1902, Theodore Roosevelt, the widely-loved President of the United States, was asked to referee in a border dispute between the states of Mississippi and Louisiana. 'Teddy', as he was nicknamed, was a big game hunter and during a break in the discussions he was invited to go on a bear hunt in Mississippi. Since no bears were shot, the embarrassed hosts invited Roosevelt to shoot a bear cub which they had tied to a tree. A humane and gentle man, the President refused to shoot because it was unsporting. News of the incident quickly reached Washington. A newspaper cartoonist, Clifford Berryman, made the political cartoon *Drawing the Line in Mississippi*.

At about the same time a Russian couple, Morris and Rose Michtom, who owned a toy shop in New York, were trying to create a soft toy for boys. The Berryman cartoon gave them the idea for a jointed plush toy bear, which they displayed in their shop window along with the cartoon and a sign saying 'Teddy's Bear'.

Above: *Clifford K Berryman's epoch-making cartoon from the Washington Evening Post, November 16, 1902.*

Right: *A young Teddy Roosevelt pictured in hunting gear, 1884.*

S*teiff* B*ear*

The Michtom's soft toy was a success and they asked Roosevelt if they could call their product 'Teddy's Bear'. The bewildered President gave his permission and the soft toy became a popular Roosevelt mascot. The Michtom's later established the Ideal Novelty and Toy Company.

However, the first soft toy bear may have actually been made in Germany. In 1877, Margarete Steiff started a dress shop in Giengen-an-der-Brenz, in southern Germany. At first she made felt underskirts but went on to experiment with felt elephant pincushions. Encouraged by her brother Fritz, she made more felt animals and a successful family business developed. In the 1890s, Fritz's son Richard introduced a new design of a soft toy bear cub based on sketches made at Stuttgart Zoo. It was not until 1903 at the Leipzig Toy Fair that the Steiff bears were 'discovered'. From 1903 to 1907, the Steiffs employed 2000 people and exported a million bears to Europe and the United States.

Left: *The Steiff bears became famous for their button-in-the-ear trademark (London Toy and Model Museum).*

Above: *Old and young Steiff bears (London Toy and Model Museum).*

Humanization

The craze for the soft toy 'Teddy's Bear' led to many cartoons and children's stories. Most of these stories shortened 'Teddy's Bear' to 'Teddy'. By 1910, soft toy bears were referred to as 'teddy bears'.

Before 1914, most teds were similar to real bears, with large hind legs, elongated snouts and humpbacks. Manufacturers in America and Europe copied the early Steiff design. The teds were stuffed with fine wood shavings and covered in the fleece of angora goats called mohair. The early teds had black boot button eyes and many had reed squeakers or growlers fitted in their stomachs. The teds became more humanized as manufacturers introduced *macho* teds wearing different costumes of the police, navy, army and circus clowns.

Below: *A nautical bear called Sampson, dating from the 1930s and housed in the London Toy and Model Museum.*

Left: *A 1911 bear dressed as a First World War German sailor, now in the Bethnal Green Museum, London.*

The Changing Ted

Between 1903 and 1914, the German toy companies dominated the world teddy market. As well as Steiff, the companies of Fleishmann and Bing introduced teds to their range of toys. With the outbreak of World War I, all German imports were banned from Britain. Without the monopoly of German toys, other countries began to develop novel teddy bears.

By the 1920s, the shape of the teddy changed into a plumper soft toy with shorter arms, large head, glass eyes and the disappearance of the humpback. Teds could be bought in different colours and were stuffed with the hygienic silk cotton fibre of kapok. The inter-war years were dominated by British toy firms including Chad Valley and Merrythought.

World War II caused European soft toy companies to change their production for the war effort. In Britain, rationing meant that hand-made knitted teds replaced manufactured bears.

Left: *A jolly group of British hand-made knitted World War II teds from the Peter Bull Collection at the London Toy and Model Museum.*

Clever Teds

....

The 1950s saw a renewed boom in manufactured teddies and all kinds of bear novelties, spurred on by the availability of new, synthetic materials and technological advancements. Hong Kong and Japan began to supply the rapidly expanding American and European markets with a wide range of cheaply-produced products. Among these were a variety of ingenious and colourful clockwork and battery-operated teddy bears. In 1955, Wendy Boston Playsafe Toys produced the first fully machine-washable ted, employing nylon plush and plastic, unbreakable eyes.

Left: *A battery-operated 'housewife' ted complete with rotating vacuum cleaner, made in Japan in the 1950s (London Toy and Model Museum).*

Right: *The Bing Skating Bear, an early clockwork bear manufactured by the German toy company, Gerbruder Bing in 1915 (London Toy and Model Museum).*

$\mathcal{P}$ i c t u r e s q u e $\mathcal{P}$ r o p

The popularity of the soft toy bear has inspired manufacturers, writers and artists. Since 1903, teddy merchandising has proliferated to include postcards, mugs, badges, tea sets, musical boxes, cartoons, puppets and books. With the rapid growth of teddy mania in the early decades of the century, the teddy bear also began his modelling career. The ted became an essential accessory in the sentimental photographic portraits of children prevalent at the time.

Left: *A grandfather's postcard to his grandson on his birthday, dated 1939 (London Toy and Model Museum).*

Right: *A selection of photographic portraits of children with their lovable and ever-loving teddy toys, from the London Toy and Model Museum.*

A.1410-4.

Mail-a-Ted

Above: *Cute and cuddly postcards from the 1930s and '40s. The card on the far left carries a Mabel Lucie Attwell illustration (London Toy and Model Museum).*

Left: *An early teddy postcard dating from 1910 (London Toy and Model Museum).*

Left: *A cheeky postcard design and an elegant French item dated 1913 (London Toy and Model Museum).*

Right: *The top postcard is an embossed variety by WM Heal, US, 1907. The two comic postcards date from the 1920s (London Toy and Model Museum).*

Mary with her little bear behind.

RUN FOR A DOCTOR QUICK! HE'S LOSING ANY AMOUNT OF SAWDUST!

BEARLY TIME TO WRITE.

Roosevelt Bears

One of the first bear-inspired series of children's stories, entitled *The Roosevelt Bears*, was created in the early 1900s by Paul Piper under the pen name of Seymour Eaton. They were originally published as serials in 20 leading daily American newspapers, but the adventures of these infamous bears soon appeared not only in books but on postcards, buttons, trays and china. The first book, *The Roosevelt Bears, Their Travels and Adventures*, was published in 1905. The Roosevelt Bears looked much more like real bears than teddies, but they made a huge impact on the soft toy bear market. They were named Teddy B, which stood for Black, and Teddy G or Gray, not Bad and Good as many people thought.

Left: *Two illustrations from* The Roosevelt Bears, Their Travels and Adventures *by Seymour Eaton. The success of the toy ted was further stimulated by 'Teddy', King Edward VII.*

Rupert Bear

Rupert Bear first appeared as a British comic strip for the *Daily Express* newspaper in 1920. Rupert was created by the children's book illustrator, Mary Tourtel. She developed fairytale stories of Rupert and his group of characterful friends - Bill Badger, Alby Pug, Edward Trunk and the Wise Old Goat - in the imaginary, idealistic town of Nutwood. The popularity of the stories was such that the *Daily Express* also published them in the form of annuals.

After Mary Tourtel's retirement in 1935 due to failing sight, Rupert continued to flourish under the pen and paintbrush of Alfred Bestall, then the team of Alex Cubie and Freddie Chaplain, and today, John Harold and Ian Robinson.

Left: *A latex Rupert Bear from the London Toy and Model Museum.*

Right: 'Those boys I'll deal with right away ...' *Cartoon frame from* Rupert and The Banjo *in the* More Rupert Adventures *annual, 1943.*

Winnie-the-Pooh

In 1924, the writer A A Milne and the illustrator E H Shepard published a collection of poems for children. One of the poems was about a tubby ted. This ted became famous from 1926 when he became Winnie-the-Pooh who had adventures with Piglet, Eeyore, Kanga and Tigger. The adventures were set in a forest based on the Ashdown Forest in southern England. Many of the stories involved Milne's son, Christopher Robin, who in reality enjoyed playing in Ashdown Forest with his teddy bear called 'Edward'. E H Shepard used his son's ted 'Growler' for his illustrations.

The curious name of Winnie-the-Pooh came from a Canadian bear and a pet swan. During the 1920s there was a bear called 'Winnie' in the London Zoo who was the mascot for the Winnipeg regiment of the Canadian army. 'Pooh' was the nickname that Christopher Robin gave to a swan.

Left: *A A Milne pictured with his son Christopher Robin and his teddy, on which the Pooh Bear stories were based.*

Right: *The Winnie-the-Pooh collection housed in the New York Public Library, including the original Pooh Bear.*

Paddington Bear

In 1958, another bear suddenly appeared at a London railway station:

'Mr and Mrs Brown first met Paddington on a railway platform. In fact, that was how he came to have such an unusual name for a bear, for Paddington was the name of the station.'

From *A Bear Called Paddington* by Michael Bond, 1958 (Collins)

This was Paddington, the bear from darkest Peru who was adopted by the Brown family despite his craving for marmalade sandwiches. Paddington was created by Michael Bond and first illustrated by Peggy Fortnum. His adventures were later made into a TV animation series.

Above: *Paddington about to meet Mrs Bird. From* A Bear Called Paddington, *illustrated by Peggy Fortnum, 1958.*

Right: *Paddington Bear, 1979 (London Toy and Model Museum).*

DARKEST PERU
TO LONDON, ENGLAND
Via PADDINGTON Stn
DARKEST REGISTRATION No. 017663

$\mathcal{A}$loysius

Even in classic English literature, teddy bears have made their appearance, as in *Brideshead Revisited* by Evelyn Waugh, when a barber describes an owner's obsession with a ted:

'What do you suppose Lord Sebastian wanted? A hair brush for his teddy-bear; it had to have very stiff bristles, not, Lord Sebastian said, to brush him with, but to threaten him with a spanking when he was sulky. He bought a very nice one with an ivory back and he's having "Aloysius" engraved on it - that's the bear's name.'

In the British television drama production of *Brideshead Revisited*, Aloysius was played by a 1907 ted loaned by the teddy collector Peter Bull, and became as successful as his human co-stars.

Right: *Jeremy Irons, Anthony Andrews and Aloysius the bear, the stars of Granada Television's production of Evelyn Waugh's* Brideshead Revisited.

$\mathcal{TV}$ $\mathcal{T}eds$

British television teds first appeared in the 1950s as puppets with Harry Corbett's *Sooty and Sweep Show*. In the late 1970s, Jim Henson created Fozzie Bear as the unbearable comedian in *The Muppet Show*. With the 1980s, Super Ted appeared in children's books by Mike Young and a successful television cartoon series was subsequently broadcast worldwide. Today, merchandizing and TV cartoons have made Rupert, Winnie-the-Pooh, Paddington and Super Ted world famous.

Right: *The inimitable Fozzie Bear, one of the Muppets created by the late Jim Henson.*

Right: *The Super Ted soft toy has a removable plush body coat, to reveal his 'working' costume and cape beneath (London Toy and Model Museum).*

Large and Small

My biggest teddy of them all
Is over four foot seven tall.
He looks most adults in the eye,
And yet he would not hurt a fly.
His name is Arthur Tompkins Bear
And sometimes he's allowed to wear
My father's best black coat and hat
And he looks oh so smart in that.
There isn't room for him in bed.
He guards me from his chair instead.
My very littlest, smallest ted
Is much too wee to come to bed.
He sleeps inside a walnut shell
Which fits around him very well.
He also has it as a boat
And wears a tiny yellow coat.
And these two bears, so large and small,
Are just the greatest friends of all.
Is one too short and one too big?
They really couldn't care a fig.

Paul Richardson

Short and Stout

Teddy Bear

A bear, however hard he tries,
Grows tubby without exercise.
Our Teddy Bear is short and fat,
Which is not to be wondered at.
But do you think it worries him
To know that he is far from slim?
No, just the other way about -
He's proud *of being short and stout.*

From *When We Were Very Young*, A A Milne, 1924
Photograph taken at the London Toy and Model Museum

Action Bear

A cheerful old bear at the zoo
Could always find something to do.
When it bored him to go
On a walk to and fro,
He reversed it, and walked fro and to

Anon

Teddy be nimble,
Teddy be quick,
Teddy jump over
The candle stick.

Traditional

Photographs taken at the London Toy and Model Museum

*B*ald *B*ear

*F*uzzy Wuzzy was a bear
A bear was Fuzzy Wuzzy.
When Fuzzy Wuzzy lost his hair
He wasn't fuzzy, was he?

Traditional

Photograph taken at the London Toy and Model Museum

Caring Bear

I heard the church bells hollowing out the sky,
Deep beyond deep, like never-ending stars,
And turned to Archibald, my safe old bear,
Whose woollen eyes looked sad or glad at me,
Whose ample forehead I could wet with tears,
Whose half-moon ears received my confidence,
Who made me laugh, who never let me down.

From *Summoned by Bells*, John Betjeman,
published by John Murray (Publishers) Ltd, 1960
Photographs opposite taken at the London Toy and
Model Museum

Teddy Bears' Picnic

If you go down in the woods today
You'd better not go alone
It's lovely down in the woods today
But safer to stay at home
For ev'ry Bear that ever there was
Will gather there for certain because
Today's the day the Teddy Bears
have their Picnic

Lyrics by Jimmy Kennedy

Sporting Bears

There was an Old Person of Ware
Who rode on the back of a Bear,
When they ask'd, 'Does it trot?'
He said, 'Certainly not!
He's a Moppsikon Floppsikon Bear!

Edward Lear

Photograph taken at the London Toy and Model Museum

$\mathcal{S}$tory $\mathcal{T}$ime

'*The three bears looked round the room. Father Bear looked at his very big chair. "Someone's been sitting in my chair," he said in a very loud voice.*'

From *Goldilocks and the Three Bears*, c 1830

'*But the bear, being very eager to see the royal palace, soon came back again, and peeping into the nest, saw five or six young birds lying at the bottom of it. "What nonsense!" said Bruin, "this is not a royal palace: I never saw such a filthy place in my life; and you are no royal children, you little base-born brats!"*'

From *The Tom-Tit and the Bear, Grimms' Fairy Tales*, 1823

Photograph taken at the London Toy and Model Museum

The Teddymobile

Y is for Yuletide
The grown people's name
For the time when my Teddy
From Santa Claus came.

Anon

Bear, Bear, don't go away
To come again some other day
I will love you if you stay
I will love you any way.

Greetings card rhyme, early 1900s
Photograph taken at the London Toy and
Model Museum

And So To Bed, Teds

Teddy bear, teddy bear turn around.
Teddy bear, teddy bear touch the ground.
Teddy bear, teddy bear go up stairs.
Teddy bear, teddy bear say your prayers.
Teddy bear, teddy bear switch off the light.
Teddy bear, teddy bear say good night.

Skipping rhyme

London Toy and Model Museum

Teddy Information

'Hugs' to visit

Bethnal Green Museum of Childhood, Cambridge Heath Road, London E2 9PA, UK. Tel: 081 980 4315

Frannie's Teddy Bear Museum, Naples, Florida, USA. Tel: 813 590 2711

London Toy and Model Museum, 21/23 Craven Hill, London W2 3EN, UK. Tel: 071 262 9450

Margaret Woodbury Strong Museum, 700 Allen Creek Road, Rochester, New York 14618, USA

Merrythought Teddy Bear Museum and Shop, Ironbridge, Telford, Shropshire, TF8 7NJ, UK.

Museum of Childhood, 42 High Street, Edinburgh, EH1 1TG, UK. Tel: 031 225 2424 ext 6645

Pollock's Toy Museum, 1 Scala Street, London, W1P 1LT, UK. Tel: 071 636 3452

Smithsonian, Washington, DC, USA

Steiff Museum, Margarete Steiff GmbH, PO Box 1560, Alliin Strasse 2, D-7928, Giengen, Germany

Teddy Bear Museum, 19 Greenhill Street, Stratford-upon-Avon, Warwickshire, CV37 6LF. Tel: 0789 293160

Teddy books

Bull, Peter *Peter Bull's Book of Teddy Bears*, Cassell, 1977

Cockrill, Pauline *The Ultimate Teddy Bear Book*, Dorling Kindersley, 1991

Fawdry, Kenneth and Marguerite *Pollock's History of English Dolls and Toys*, Ernest Benn Ltd, 1979

Mullins, Linda *Teddy Bears Past and Present: A Collector's Identification Guide*, Hobby House Press, 1987

Opie, James *The Letts Guide to Collecting 20th Century Toys*, Charles Letts, 1991

Pearson, Sue *Teddy Bears*, Silent Books, 1990

Teddy magazines

The UK Teddy Bear Guide, annual directory of teddy artists, restorers and shops. Published by

Hugglets, PO Box 290. Brighton BN2 1DR, UK
Hugglets Teddy Bear Magazine, four issues a year published by Hugglets
The Teddy Bear Times, four issues a year published by Ashdown Publishing, 104 High Street, Steyning, West Sussex BN4 3RD, UK
The Teddy Tribune, 254 West Sidney Street, St Paul, Minnesota 55107, USA
Teddy Bear and Friends, 900 Frederick Street, Cumberland, Maryland 21502, USA
Teddy Bear Review, 170 Fifth Avenue, New York, NY 10010, USA

Teddy restoration and commissions
British Toymakers Guild, 124 Walcot Street, Bath, Avon BA1 5BG. Tel:0225 442440. Members of the Guild restore and produce "one-off" teds for commission.